Sleepy Book

Charlotte Zolotow

illustrations by Ilse Plume

Harper & Row, Publishers

To my mother
C.Z.

To Alice Plume
Ilse

Sleepy Book
Text copyright © 1958 by Charlotte Zolotow
Text copyright renewed 1986 by Charlotte Zolotow
Illustrations copyright © 1988 by Ilse Plume
Originally published by Lothrop, Lee & Shepard
Printed in
the United States of America. For information address
Harper & Row Junior Books, 10 East 53rd Street,
New York, N.Y. 10022. Published simultaneously in
Canada by Fitzhenry & Whiteside Limited, Toronto.
10 9 8 7 6 5 4 3 2 1
Newly Illustrated Edition

Library of Congress Cataloging-in-Publication Data
Zolotow, Charlotte, 1915–
   Sleepy Book.

   Summary: Describes how each animal sleeps in its own
special place, in its own special way.
   1. Sleep—Juvenile literature.   [1. Sleep.
2. Animals—Habits and behavior]   I. Title.
QP425.Z65 1988   [E]   87-45861
ISBN 0-06-026967-7
ISBN 0-06-026968-5 (lib. bdg.)

Sleepy Book

Bears
sleep
in
their
dark
caves
the long
winter
through.

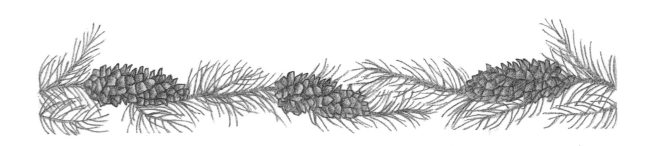

Pigeons
sleep
in
a row
pressing
against
each other
for
warmth.

Fish sleep
among
the green
water ferns
with
their eyes
and mouths
wide
open.

Moths
sleep
with wings
folded together.
They look like
little
white leaves
on walls
and windows
and screens.

Horses
sleep
standing up
in fields
and stalls
their tails
switching
to keep away
the flies.

Seals
sleep
with
their
flippers
flat
against
blocks of
ice.

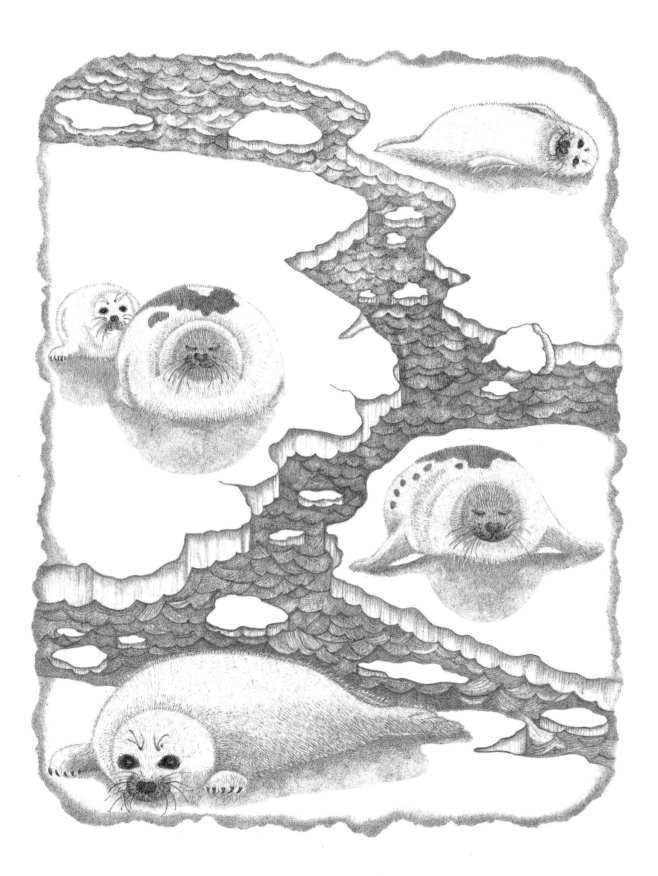

The snowy
crane
sleeps
standing
on one long
leg
like
a flower
on its stem.

Crickets
sleep in
the long
meadow grass
and look
like the grass
itself—
they are
so still.

Turtles
sleep in
their
shells
and no one
would know
a turtle
was there.

Caterpillars
sleep in
their
silky
cocoons.

Spiders
when
they sleep
are like
small
ink spots
in the
middle of
their
lacy webs.

Kittens
sleep
in the warmest
place
they can find—
curled up
in a basket or
stretched out
purring
in the sun.

Dogs
sleep
under beds
or in boxes
or on rugs
near
someone
they
like.

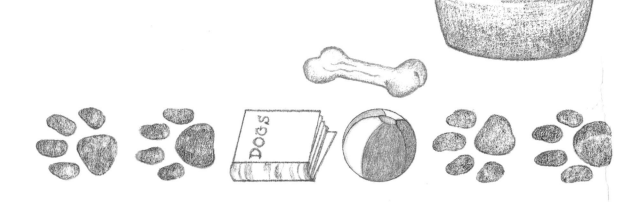

But little boys
and girls,
when the night
comes
and the wind
whispers gently
in the trees
and the stars
sparkle and shine,
sleep
warm under
their blankets
in their
beds